A SENIOR SMART HOUSE

~ The Home that Cares for You ~

Mrs. Teri Lyn Vander Heiden

A Senior Smart House: A Home that Cares for You
Founder, Author & Copyright © 2023 by Mrs. Teri Lyn Vander Heiden
Photographers: Gunter Nezhoda
Artist: Ozzy Zillate

ISBN:

Paperback: 978-1959151661

e-book: 978-1959151678

The Reading Glass
BOOKS

The Reading Glass Books
+1 (888) 420-3050
production@readingglassbooks.com

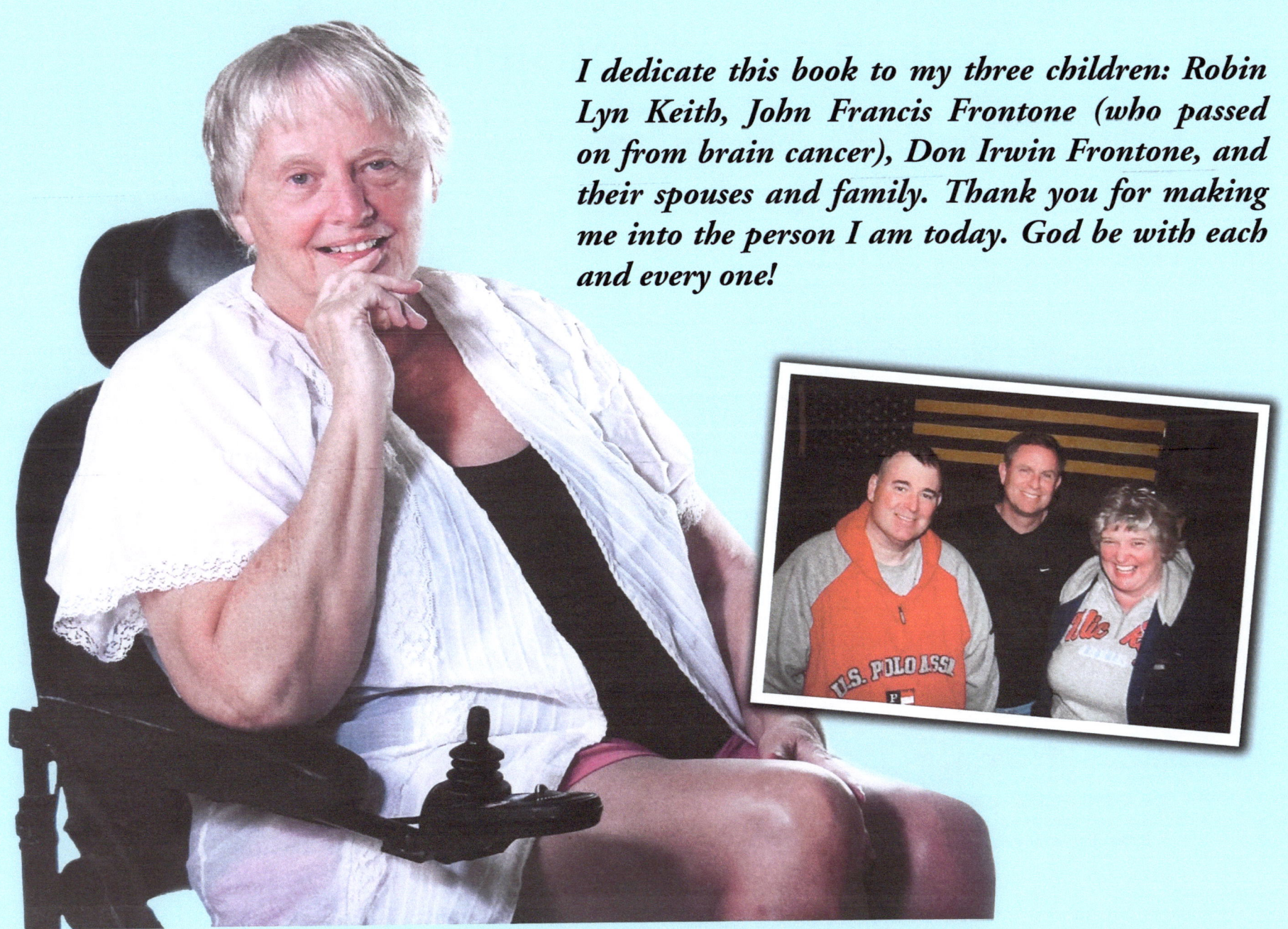

I dedicate this book to my three children: Robin Lyn Keith, John Francis Frontone (who passed on from brain cancer), Don Irwin Frontone, and their spouses and family. Thank you for making me into the person I am today. God be with each and every one!

SENIOR SMART HOUSE UPDATE

The update includes living in this home for 10 years and experienced the changes that happened with age and use of items in my home. I will let you know about the following:

1. The gas fireplace was removed due to a residue of gray smoke on the wall that became unbearable.
2. My ceiling lights were too many and to replace them when needed replaced, after burning out, hiring service people was not something that was in the plan.
3. Replacing a nuwave stove top that quit working after 5 years. Contacting repair people found out this model top was no longer available.
4. Under-counter refrigerators broke down over 5-10 years. I had to replace all of them. Now using them for storage. Each frig costs over $1000.
5. Alexa was a new item that regulated many things. Smart lights are a blessing since you can turn them on and off by asking her to do that. Great to have her answer questions about anything. Quick with answers.
6. Replaced the gray water tank with a new tank that runs water directly into the septic tank—where water was running low in our city.
7. The patio floor was cement, painted coral and dust was beginning to be difficult to keep clean. I decided to lay cement tiles, and gray planks, which are easy to clean and never see dust.

As I review the repairs and replacements, having lived in this house since 2013, I am learning many new ways to live!

I first had to repair my under-counter refrigerator but could not locate repair people to do repairs. I contacted the main company and they sent me a new refrigerator. So I was surprised that this frig had to be replaced two more times. Finally bought a tall inexpensive refrigerator with a top freezer which has lasted through all the replacement refrigerators.

The company of these $1000 refrigerators wanted me to dump the broken frigs. I have them used as storage drawers. Most expensive storage in town!

I did build two sliding drawers where one frig was and used it for large pots and bottles. One has to reinvent being practical. At my age, 88, at this writing, I work hard at thinking up normal, common ways to live in my home.

When designing the kitchen, I had the front of all drawers cut open to see what was in each drawer since I could not remember what was behind closed drawers. I have to keep each drawer neat this way. The new stove top was wonderful, but after 5 years, it quit. They no longer sell that model, so I have to replace the stove top with a top that the burner gets hot when using them, so I have to be extra careful not to burn myself. My microwave has been substitute to cooking then my roommate did a wonderful for cooking a new house to keep from getting burned. Since he died two years ago, I have used the microwave to cook frozen meals. Finding new ways on how to use an air fryer. Also, I can use fresh mushrooms and spinach to create an interesting breakfast.

The 41 ceiling lights were another problem. I would have to use a serviceman to change light bulbs on a high ladder. So went to Applebees one day and saw their hanging lights and decided. They could be used as drop-down lights in my kitchen, office, bedroom, and hallway. So installed several to make it easier to replace burnt our bulbs with a low ladder. As time flys by, I find new things to help my old age problems to be manageable.

Alexa is wonderful! She turns on/off my lights in rooms before I get to the room! I haven't looked into all the new things she can do but I suggest you try them if you have things that can help you live comfortably in your home. For a senior, security aids can be wonderful! I see where great improvements by Alexa can help you.

The gas fireplace built with this house turned out to be a problem with the black smoke marking the wall and had to be washed off. Decided to remove the gas and put in a motion flame fireplace turned on by a remote control. Home Depot sells them and no dirty walls now. Even has a fan to blow warm air and enjoy the flames. No work in my old age to cut wood or clean our ashes.

Each month I check any repairs to this Senior Smart House, but toilets began to be a problem.

I have three! I was told they should be checked every 5 years and new parts be put in the tanks. Had to recheck the new parts due to the constant running of water in the tanks. Once we knew how to regulate water in the tank, no more running! So if I live another 5 years, I can replace parts again. Hopefully, my old mind will remember. Photos of my repair items are included.

I still welcome visitors when you are in Las Vegas to walk through this home and take photos to help you with your home!

The parking area for visitors.

WELCOME TO THE SENIOR SMART HOUSE—*THE HOME THAT CARES FOR YOU! A PROTOTYPE HOME FOR A HANDICAPPED PERSON TO LIVE IN AND ENJOY AND FEEL INDEPENDENT IN.*

As a widow, in 2003, I had a problem sleeping! I began napping in my recliner and having (what I call) twilight dreams! While resting, I would hear inner voices telling me all kinds of things I did not understand! So after several days, I began writing down what I heard, which filled a few spiral pads with things I didn't understand.

I shared these pads with a friend who knew about building homes, and he told me I was designing a "smart home"! He introduced me to a couple of owners with this style of home. Now understand, I am a widow, on a pension, and I own my own older home, which needed to be remodeled to sell. When I visited the "smart home" of his friends, they were millionaires! Way out of my pocketbook! Seeing these homes and reading my notes, I found that there were similarities in content. The only problem was a wheelchair used in these homes would be difficult to get around in, even with the elevator! I decided a one-story home, with special doors, bathrooms, etc., would be nice for me to live out my old age in! Now understand, I am a widow, on a pension, and I own my older home, needing to be remodeled to sell.

For the next several years, I began to listen to my voices (angels or spiritual guides guiding me) since I had never built a house only remodeled a few and as a licensed Real Estate Broker and owner of two R.E. offices, I sold, listed, rented properties, but build? Oh, boy, that was not in my head but it began to come from my heart! Note: IF YOU HAVE A DREAM, FOLLOW IT! While remodeling a room a year of my 1974, 5 bedroom, 3 bath home in hope to sell it by 2010, I found an architect designer to use my drawings for County approval. I then found a contractor to get me started on this new adventure! It has been an interesting ten years.

Then when my house was completed and approved by Clark County inspectors, for occupancy, I had my friend John Bear bless this new home on April 1, 2011. My inner voice was telling me I had to cleanse the space of all negative energy! Four years later I am so glad I did! Visitors tell me they have special feelings while visiting and walking throughout the home.

When I was remodeling the old house, my fiftieth class reunion was held in Wellsville, Ohio. I decided to drive across country to visit family and friends along the way. When I went to my class meeting to visit with old classmates and friends I remet Igor Sedor who I had not seen for fifty-two years! When he found out I lived in Las Vegas while he lived in California, he wanted to come and visit me when we return home. A month later he came to visit and hasn't left! He has helped me (due to medical issues) and we are good friends that help each other. (As of this writing, I am eighty and he is eighty-two.) Our families are happy we help each other living in the new SENIOR SMART HOUSE. He makes beautiful Native American-style flutes, for 25 years. I had enough land to design and build a studio/workshop next to the house. He was married twice and friends with his former wives. I had been married four times to wonderful men, widowed twice through cancer and accident in 2003. These past 10 years have been most interesting due to the many unique people we have had the privilege to meet!

With this unusual home you are viewing in this book, the concept of using the Eastern/Western philosophies, of universal energies, has been the theme. To help one live in a healing home, with the energy of color to give a person the chi energy that gives one lots of life!

The SENIOR SMART HOUSE concept, you are viewing and visiting help you to feel the FENG SHUI (uniqueness) from a traditional home in which most people live. We invite you to view and enjoy the photos and descriptions of what they represent! Looking forward to meeting with you soon! God be with you and your dreams, whatever they may be.

Senior Living

As a senior widow, I've designed my home to care for me. There are so many wonderful "toys" for the senior that are affordable and you can live green, and your utilities can be less than you may be paying now.

I found this technology easy to use, even for a novice computer user. Now with my Senior Smart Home, I can be visiting my children out of state and use my computer to check my home, turn things on or off, and secure my house—all from a thousand miles away!

I am working to make this project affordable to retirees who don't want to move into assisted-living facilities or impose on children or grandchildren. There is a variety of packages to provide for individual needs and to assist in making you safe and secure in your home.

Taking Care of You

This unique system takes care of you with thoughtful designs and technology to make everyday activities easy for anyone.

Do you need lights turned on but can't find the lamp? Smart lights go on when you walk in the room, and off when you leave.

Have trouble turning on water faucets? Use smart plumbing fixtures that turn on by putting your hands under the faucet. The water cools and warms by touch. Take your hand away, and the water turns off.

PELLA windows are through out the home. Double glass, sliding doors, and windows have blinds within them. Blinds can be washed every 3-5 years by opening inside window. Easy to wipe glass to save on labor of all these windows, which when opened allow for cross ventilation for the home.

Sensors throughout the home will notify designated persons or agencies in case you fall or become ill and require medical help. This system does not need to be monitored by the monthly-fee companies, but it can be.

Come Visit Me

In my lifetime, I've seen fantastic changes throughout the world, especially in electronics. As a young woman, I was the very last Ohio Bell Telephone operator to work on a phone board—**Ah**, the times have changed!

I've been dreaming of a home that will take care of me. I've toured lots of homes with many specialized rooms that do wonderful things for you. My desire is to stay in my home for as long as possible and not rely on family, neighbors, or go into an assisted-living facility. To that end, I've selected the following for my house: lighting control, air-conditioning control, automated help for medical care, shade control.

I will be testing the pros and cons of each of these components during normal daily living. The contractors and companies who put my home together for my comfort can update any future improvements.

The house was completed on April 1, 2011 and visitors are welcome by appointment. I'll walk you through a total hands-on demonstration of the Senior Smart Home and, if you're interested, put you in touch with the contractors.

While building and designing this home I used the KISS METHOD "KEEP IT SIMPLE, SWEETLY!" I invite you to come and experience the magic in this house!

Located at 555 Rossmore Drive, Las Vegas, Nevada 89110.
(702) 577-3127
nareteri@aol.com

Artificial grass and several metal colorful flowers are mixed with real ones are around the yard.

The outside patio in the evening has rope lights that represents water.

Hummingbird on the Front Gates.

Sunset from the
Senior Smart House.

The gray water tank was put in for re-use of water for irrigating the live plants in the yard. I suggest they consider for new homes to recycle due to drought conditions in the west.

This is where the second tank was put after disconnecting the first gray tank. (used for holding water used in the house). With water levels low in Las Vegas, thought reusing water from showers, dish water, laundry would be helping yard plants. But found out 1-2 people did not use enough water and had to add water from our hose to keep the tank full. It is better when you have more than 3 people in the house.

A mural by Ozzie, of Redrock Canyon, Mt. Charleston and Lake Mead is painted on the back wall off the patio. This brings memories of the real places when you set and watch the sun sets over Las Vegas, and the morning sun raises, which can be very pink and beautiful!

FAMILY ROOM/KITCHEN: The kitchen has a touch faucet; under counter drawer refrigerators; a nu wave stove top. All cupboards are open to see contents, aids in forgetfulness. Bamboo floors are throughout the house (represents the earth).

HEART OF THE HOME IS THE OFFICE: Wine colored wall has the history photos of my family. (Chi energy represents richness of life).

(Gray wall Chi energy represents active life), so events are posted on this wall!

This room has the tools for security cameras, solar montoring, computers for communicating, in many ways. The sky light is a tube which a 2 nd tube is in the small room above the garage, where hot water and cooling systems are located.

Pella windows have blinds between glass easy to clean.

All colors used, gathered, chi-energy learned from Feng Shui eastern knowledge. Painted sky/clouds: colors- green, aqua, red, yellow, pink, etc, with bamboo floors are the western philosophies.

Family room, red wall is the energy of life.

A bedroom/sitting room, sleep at night and enjoy during the day. Chi energy (light green) it helps one heal, then rest and enjoy peace.

The two main bathrooms are made of Kera Glass, a form of cultured marble that is poured into molds to give the sinks, and shower, easy cleaning! No joints to clean, is nice! The shower floors have texture for nonslip, which is very nice for safety.

The meditation room, is located off the patio in the back of the house. This room is aquamarine, for Chi, water color. When you set in this room, look out to the patio, mural, this area gives you peace and healing not found anywhere else in the home. It has given several visitors fantastic feelings if they came to visit for an hour! They would relax, and if something had been bothering them, it was gone within the hour.

The garage has a painted gold ceiling with multiple colors around this room. It is also set up with heat and cooling. The room is used for various events held for those interested in music, sales, life, etc. The Founder opens this house daily to encourage others to learn about how a home can care for you.

The pantry/storage is next to the garage for easy access.

The weeping willow in the picture is the sacred tree, for healing, of the Native American Indian.

This is the living room, the entry to the home. The front door glass is a security glass, you can see out, the person cannot see in from the outside. Two side doors are screened only for fresh air. The entry to the garage and the pantry is from the living room.

Sensors are placed throughout the house. When moving around at night, in a wheelchair, lights go on/off. Using an IPOD/IPAD lights, heat/air can be turn on/off and also security cameras can be turned on when away from the property!

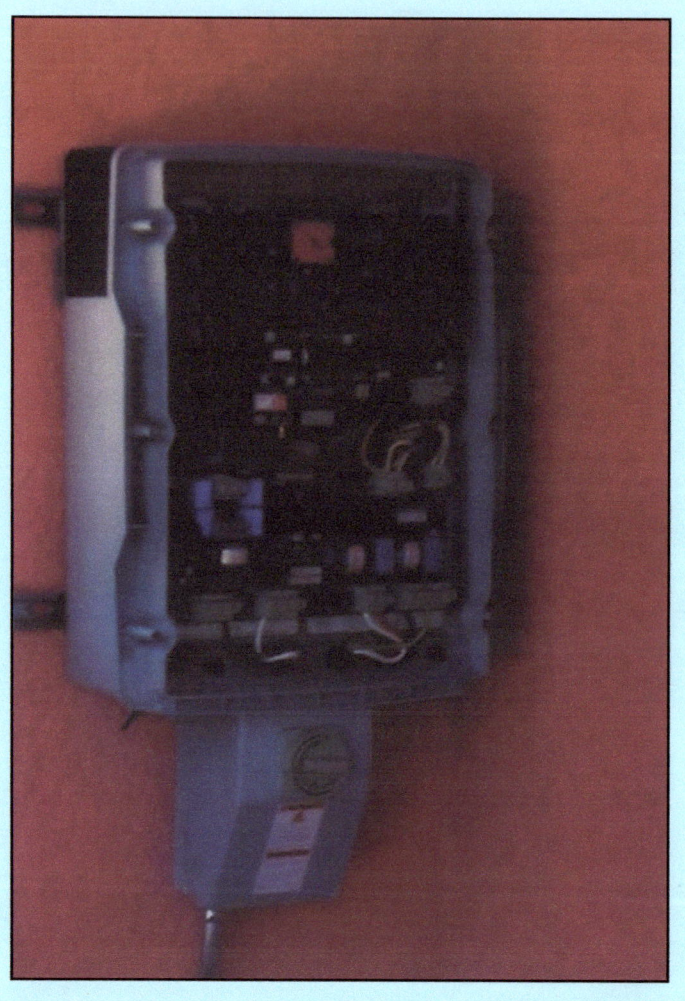

30 Solar panels assist with energy for the Senior Smart House. Since installing these panels in June 2014, the power bills per month have been under 25 dollars prior to not having panels.

This is the Smart Box that operates the 30 panels before it connects to the local energy.

The studio workshop where Igor Sedor makes his Native American style flutes. He calls his style flute Echo Quest and he teaches those people wanting to know how to make a Native American flute and also how to play it.

Igor has been a friend of Teri's since high school. Igor is now 82 and has been making these flutes for over 25 years.

Teri Lyn with her high school buddy Igor Sedor 52 years later. He was the topic of my first book, Igor and his Roadrunner "Buddy", a true story.

Igor came in 2005 to visit and never left!

Biography

Teri Lyn Vander Heiden

Teri Lyn was born in East Liverpool, Ohio, on February 18, 1935. She's been married four times and widowed twice. Teri has been blessed with three children (two sons, John and Don, and daughter Robin), thirteen grandchildren, and 20+ great-grandchildren. She has been a masseuse all her life and found she possessed a healing touch and a calling to help others.

Teri has always been involved in the community. At Fremont Junior High School in Mesa, Arizona, she worked as a multi-media assistant. She has served as a health and safety coordinator for an underground gold and silver mine in Virginia City, Nevada. She held the offices of president of the Real Estate Board at Incline Village, Lake Tahoe and Northern Nevada Real Estate Commissioner and was the broker/owner of two real estate offices (Lake Tahoe and Las Vegas). Teri retired in 2003 due to an accident in which her husband died.

Teri lost her eldest son, John, to brain cancer in 2009.

"Prayer has been my top priority. John was a special child of God. He will not be forgotten, an angel of God."

Photo and Makeup by Gayle Beverly
(www.gaylebeverly.weebly.com)

Photo and Makeup by Gayle Beverly
(www.gaylebeverly.weebly.com)

The Professional Photographer for this Book

Gunter Nezhoda was born in Vienna, Austria, lived 10 years in Frankfurt, Germany and moved to Las Vegas, NV in 1990. He spent years of his life being a musician and has recorded on Bass with guitar heroes like *Pat Travers, Leslie West, Michael Schenker, George Lynch* etc.

His photography was used by clients such as *Microsoft, Big-O Tires, Ford* and many others and was featured in countless magazines and ads. His portraits are known for their high impact and the capability of Gunter to get any expression on a clients face he wants too, and always clicks in the right moment.

http://gunter-nezhoda.artistwebsites.com/
https://www.facebook.com/gunter.nezhoda

Ozzy Villate, artist extraordinaire, painted the sky throughout the interior of this house. He painted the beautiful weeping willow tree (the holy tree of the Native American Indians) in the living room entry. He refinished the exterior mural of Red Rock, Mount Charleston, and Lake Mead, locatewd on the lower back wall.

Ozzy was born in Havana, Cuba. At the age of four, his parents came to America in pursuit of a brighter future for his family. Art was intriguing him from a young age, and he was influenced by his uncle's paintings. In grade school, he received much admiration from his teachers and students! He had three years in architectural design in a trade/tech high school.

He had a twenty-year lapse due to worldly travels and endeavors, as was the case of the prodigal son! Inspired by his renewed faith, he enrolled in the fine arts program at UNLV and has reached his own course of exploration of light and color! His vibrant colors and designs are very unique and exciting! His murals appear all around Las Vegas. In the past seven years, he has commissioned paintings in the Tuscany Suites & Casino, Smith Center, Rainbow Casino in Henderson, and several private properties. You are welcome to see his murals at the Senior Smart House, located at 555 Rossmore Drive, Las Vegas, Nevada.

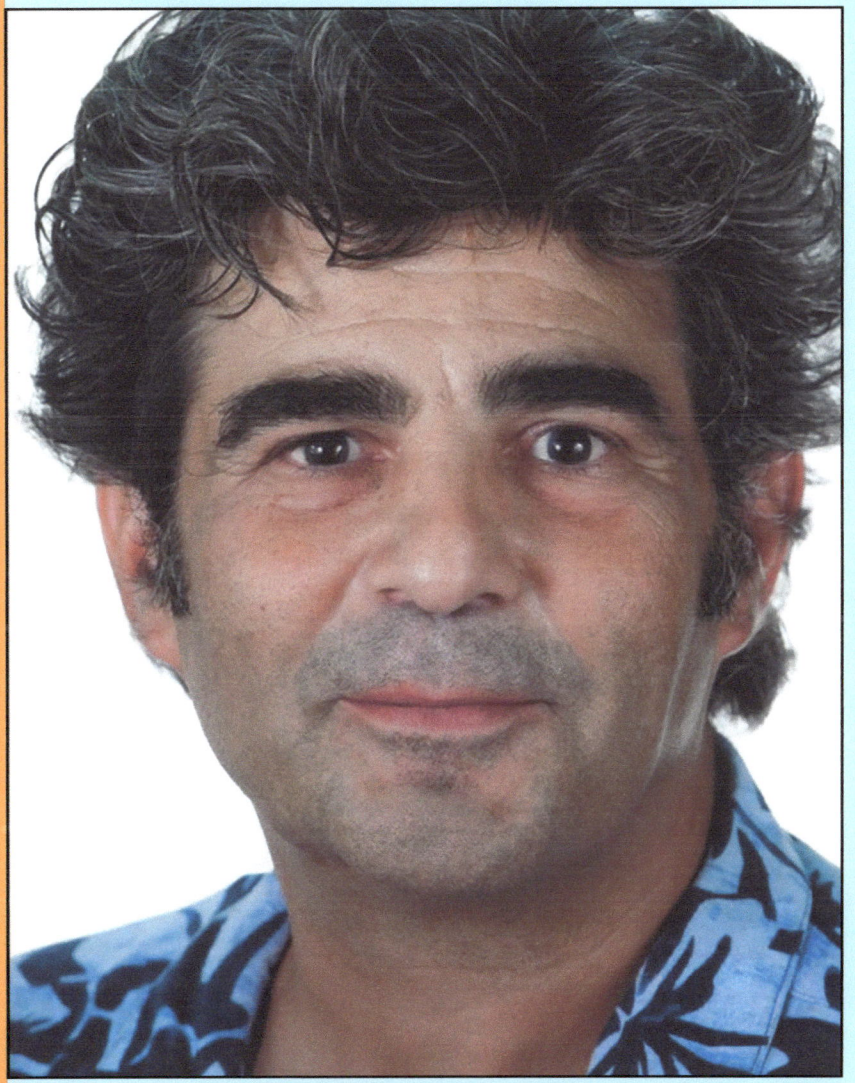

2014—private commissions, paintings, and murals. Decorative faux finishing-residential and commercial.

2013—Smith Center, Children's Discovery Museum, scenic murals at three exhibits, WaterWorld, Toddler Town, Who Dun It. Private commissions, paintings, and murals, decorative faux finishing.

2012—commissioned paintings for hotel, Tuscany Suites & Casino, Las Vegas, Nevada. Prints and installs for seven hundred suites.

2010—private commission, paintings, murals, decorative faux finishing.

2009—Promise Mural of Rainbow Casino, Water Street, Henderson, Nevada. Tuscany ceiling of wedding chapel.

2008—Zap 2, Paradise Park (electric boxes), Clark County commission. Private commissions, paintings, and murals.

A
Senior Smart House

The Home that Cares for You!

A **"Thank you"** to *all* persons and corporations assisting in making A senior widow's dream come true!

To all visitors wanting information on the construction of this home, any items utilized throughout the home can be found within this booklet!

May this dream reach out to many in remembering KISS: *keep it simple sweetly!*

Thank you to all the many people involved with the
building of this Senior Smart House—The Home that Cares for You!

AC HOUSTON;
ADVANCED DESIGN;
ADRIAN BENGT BENI MADJAR;
AMSA CONTRACTORS, INC.;
ANGLE ENGINEERING;
AUTOMATIC DOOR & GLASS CO.;
AVANTI MASONRY;

JOHN BEARINGSIDE-Blessed this home with an Indian
Ceremony & designed the iron fence and gates
BILL BUDD PLUMBING;
BOMBARD RENEWABLE ENERGY SOLAR PANELS;

CACTI LANDSCAPE;
CLARK COUNTY INSPECTORS;
CHANNEL 8 NEWS NOW;

DESERT LUMBER;
DESERT TRUSS;

DIRECT BUY;
DOOR SOLUTIONS OF NEVADA;
DRC-SURVEYOR;

Free dirt donated by HOOLIHAN'S-Michael
& EVAN'S EXCAVATION-Jerry;
FIRE & ICE;

FRIENDS & FAMILY (SPECIAL THANKS),
IGOR SEDOR,
DON FRONTONE,
BILL MILLER, CARLENE BOWDEN, JUDY PRESTOW,
STEPHAN & ROBIN KEITH;

GUNTER NEZHODA-Professional Photographer

HARRON CONSTRUCTION;
HOME DEPOT;

ITT TECHNOLOGY STUDENTS;

KERA GLASS COMPANY;
KILCHENKO, LIDA-ARTIST
LAWLER, WALTER, Artistic Engineer
LIFE SOURCE
LOWES-Charleston
LV REVIEW JOURNAL;
LV ROOFING SUPPLY;

MARTIN GARAGE DOORS
M&T MAINTENANCE, LLC;
MORGAN STANLEY;

NV ENERGY;
8 NEWS NOW;

PELLA WINDOWS;

ROCK CITY;

SCHLAGE:
SEATTLELUX-MAX MAILBOX;
STATEWIDE FIRE PROTECTION;
SUMMIT APPLIANCES;

THE SLIDING DOOR COMPANY;

UC CONSTRUCTION & SPECIALIZED WORKMEN;
UNLV PROFESSORS (Green-TECH suggestions);

OZZIE VILLATE-Artist

WHITE CAP

For those of you not mentioned, I apologize for not remembering who you are! I just appreciate all that you have done, in completing this 'one of kind' home, that heals each person visiting, encourages those with dreams. Thank you ALL & God Bless You for MY DREAM!

Teri L. Vander Heiden
nareteri@aol.com

Mural on the Back Wall

Red Rock, Mt. Charleston, Lake Meade

Enjoying the view of important places in Nevada from my patio.